This is the First Holy Communion book of

_____

A gift from _____

I was baptized at _____

on _____

My godparents are

_____

_____

I first came to the table of the Lord

at _____ on _____

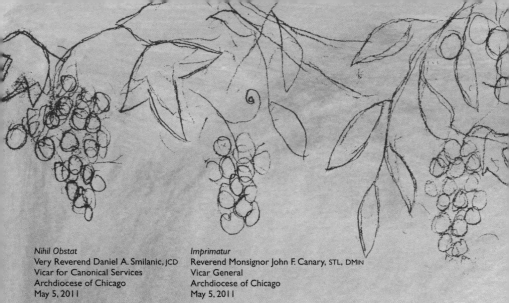

Nihil Obstat
Very Reverend Daniel A. Smilanic, JCD
Vicar for Canonical Services
Archdiocese of Chicago
May 5, 2011

Imprimatur
Reverend Monsignor John F. Canary, STL, DMIN
Vicar General
Archdiocese of Chicago
May 5, 2011

Dedicated to the Catholic Community at Colorado College. Sursum corda!

Prayer texts on pages 55 through 64, except as noted, are reprinted from *Catholic Household Blessings and Prayers* © 1988 United States Catholic Conference, Inc., Washington DC. All rights reserved. Used with permission. The translation of the Magnificat on page 62 is by Anne Carter. Text © 1988 Society of the Sacred Heart. Excerpts from the English translation of *The Roman Missal* © 2010, International Commission on English in the Liturgy Corporation (ICEL); excerpts from the English translation of *The Liturgy of the Hours* © 1974, ICEL; the English translation of the *Anima Christi* and the Prayer to the Guardian Angel from *A Book of Prayers* © 1982, ICEL. All rights reserved. The English translation of the *Gloria Patri* by the International Consultation on English Texts.

MY FIRST HOLY COMMUNION: SUNDAY MASS AND DAILY PRAYERS, REVISED EDITION © 2011 Liturgy Training Publications, 3949 South Racine Avenue, Chicago IL 60609; 1-800-933-1800, fax 1-800-933-7094, orders@ltp.org. Web site: www.LTP.org.

Printed in the United States of America.

Library of Congress Control Number: 2011931442

ISBN 978-1-61671-041-5
HCOM2

LTP

LITURGY
TRAINING
PUBLICATIONS

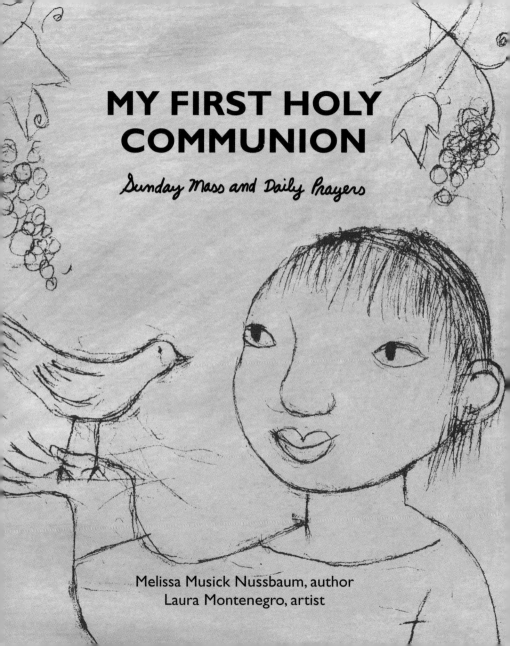

MY FIRST HOLY COMMUNION

Sunday Mass and Daily Prayers

Melissa Musick Nussbaum, author
Laura Montenegro, artist

To you who are now coming to the table of the Lord:

From the day of your Baptism, the Church prepared a place for you at the table of the Lord.

Every Sunday the baptized people gather around this table. And now you are called to come to that table, to taste and see the goodness of the Lord.

On the table are bread and wine. The good earth gives us wheat and gives us grapes.

Women and men harvest the wheat and grind it into flour and make bread. Men and women harvest the grapes and crush them and pour the juice into barrels, where it turns into wine.

So the table is set with gifts that earth has given and human hands have made. We pray that God will send the Holy Spirit upon these gifts so that the bread and wine become, for us, the Body and Blood of Christ.

Christ is our food. Christ is our drink.
All the hungry, thirsty Church is called
to eat and drink at the table of the Lord.
We pray that God will send us out to
be the Body of Christ for the world.

You come to this table with your
brothers and sisters. Sunday after
Sunday, for as long as you live, you
will raise your voice in song. You will
turn your ear to hear the story. You will
pray for those in need. You will offer
your hands in peace. You will walk in
procession to the table of the Lord.
You will do the loving work of Christ
in the world.

This book will help you find your way.
Learn by heart the words we say and
sing together.

Learn by heart the processions and the
gestures and the stillness that are part
of Sunday Mass.

Welcome to the table!

Have you ever seen a quilt?

Do you have a quilt?

Whether large or small, a quilt is made
of many tiny pieces of cloth.

Red pieces, blue pieces,
cotton pieces, silk pieces.

A quilt can be made of old baby clothes
or worn-out blue jeans
or brand new squares of fabric
fresh from the shop.

Think of all the work that goes into a quilt.

Someone gathers different kinds
and colors of cloth.

cloth scr

Someone cuts the cloth
into triangles or circles or squares.

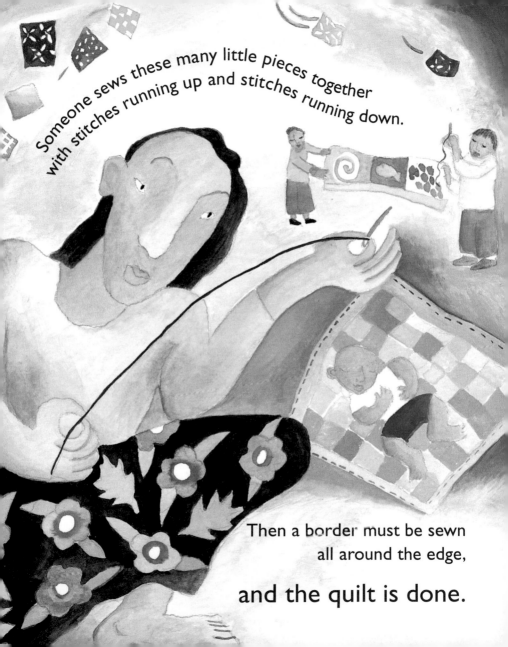

Someone sews these many little pieces together
with stitches running up and stitches running down.

Then a border must be sewn
all around the edge,

and the quilt is done.

No one could stay warm under
a single scrap of cotton.

No one could wrap a child in
one small square of flannel.
But a whole quilt is thick and warm.

A quilt will protect you from the cold.

We can cuddle in a quilt
when we are lonely.

A quilt may bring us
sweet dreams.

A quilt will cover a bed
like a bright spill of flowers.

A quilt will lie on your
shoulders like a royal robe.

Every Sunday we gather for Mass.

Our journey to church begins at home.

Many people wake up early to wash and dress.
Others try for a little extra sleep.
Someone feeds the baby.
Someone helps us find socks that match
and gets all the shoelaces tied tight.

Perhaps we stop along the way to church
and bring neighbors or grandparents with us.

We are all like the pieces of a quilt
coming together.

This is our feast day.
We want to join hands,
to sing and to speak.

We come into church, all of us together.
We greet one another and begin to visit.

We ask about someone who is sick,
about a new baby, a trip,
the first day of school,
a missing tooth,
a job found, a job lost.

We look around and see the splashes of color and size
and shape spreading throughout the church.

In the name of the Father, and of the Son,
and of the Holy Spirit. Amen.

We begin to sing.
We keep time.
We keep rhythm.

Some of us walk
carrying the cross
and the candles
and our special book.

The song draws us
shoulder to shoulder,
hand to hand.

Our singing is like a thread
weaving up and down
and in and out,
stitching us together.

The Lord be with you.
And with your spirit.

We pray.

We give thanks to God for bringing us
from the east and the west,
from the north and the south,
from houses and apartments,
from shelters and the street
to this good place.

One God, forever and ever. Amen.

We sit quietly now because we want to hear our stories.
We want to hear how God spoke
and the world was created.
We want to hear how God called a people.

We want to hear surprising news, good news:
Even when the people forgot God,
God remembered them, always.

The book of readings is something
like a crazy quilt made up of
stories, poems, letters and visions.
This book is our treasure.

The word of the Lord. Thanks be to God.

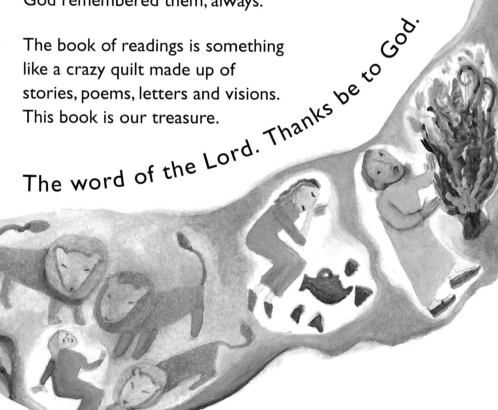

We stand up and sing out our Alleluia.
We are getting ready to hear the Gospel.

 Glory to you, O Lord.

We hear how Jesus came
to show us what God looks like.

God looks like a shepherd
leaving many sheep behind in order to search
the fields for one missing lamb.

God looks like a woman with ten silver coins.
When she loses one, she sweeps her whole house
searching for the coin.
And when she finds her lost treasure,
she calls all her friends to gather and rejoice.

Praise to you, Lord Jesus Christ.

We think of all the people, men and women, children and adults, all over the world.

God is stitching us, piece to piece, need to plenty, strength to weakness, sorrow to joy.

Now we stand again. We pray for the world.

We pray for the poor and for the Church everywhere.

We pray for the sick. We pray for the dead.

We pray for those we will never meet,
whose names we will never know.

God knows each one by name.
So we can sing, "Lord, hear our prayer."

Lord, have mercy.
Christ, have mercy.
Lord, have mercy.

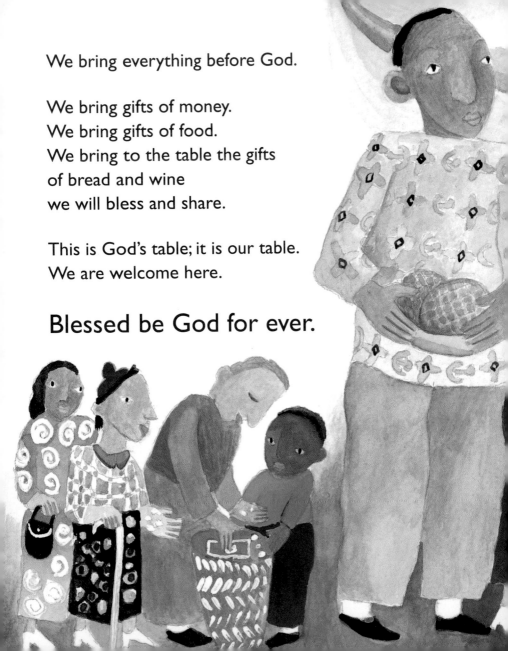

We bring everything before God.

We bring gifts of money.
We bring gifts of food.
We bring to the table the gifts
of bread and wine
we will bless and share.

This is God's table; it is our table.
We are welcome here.

Blessed be God for ever.

Now the priest calls to us: "Lift up your hearts."

 We lift them up to the Lord.

We begin our praise to God for all the wonders God
has done and is doing in our sight, in our hearing,
in our bread and wine, in flesh and blood.

Holy, Holy, Holy God Lord of hosts.
Heaven and earth are full of your glory.
Hosanna in the highest.
Blessed is he who comes in the name
        of the Lord.
Hosanna in the highest.

"You are indeed Holy, O Lord," we proclaim
with Christians throughout the world,
"and you never cease to gather a people
        to yourself,
so that from the rising of the sun to
        its setting
a pure sacrifice may be offered
        to your name."

Hosanna in the highest.

We lift up our hearts and sing of Christ.
He is the Word through whom you made the universe,
the Savior you sent to redeem us.

By the Holy Spirit
he took flesh and was born of the Virgin Mary.

For our sake he opened his arms on the cross;
he put an end to death and revealed his Resurrection.

The priest prays to God:
"May this same Holy Spirit
graciously sanctify these offerings."

Then we remember what Jesus did
and how he loved us.

He took bread, blessed and broke it,
and gave it to his disciples, saying:

"TAKE THIS, ALL OF YOU, AND EAT OF IT,
FOR THIS IS MY BODY,
WHICH WILL BE GIVEN UP FOR YOU."

He also took the cup.
He gave you thanks and praise,
gave the cup to his disciples, and said:

"TAKE THIS, ALL OF YOU, AND DRINK FROM IT,
FOR THIS IS THE CHALICE OF MY BLOOD."

We proclaim your Death, O Lord,
and profess your Resurrection
until you come again.

Save us, Savior of the world,
for by your Cross and Resurrection
you have set us free.

We thank God that we are able
to stand before him and serve him.
We pray that all who receive
Holy Communion are united
by the Holy Spirit.

Amen!

We cannot keep from singing:
Amen! Amen! Amen! Amen! Amen!
"Yes, and again, yes," we sing.

Always and forever.
"Yes," we sing, "may it be so."

We sing our Amen
until it spins out into the heavens,
like bright thread
joining all the Amens over all the earth.

Our Father, who art in heaven,
hallowed be thy name;
thy kingdom come,
thy will be done
on earth as it is in heaven.

Give us this day our daily bread,
and forgive us our trespasses,
as we forgive those
        who trespass against us;
and lead us not into temptation,
but deliver us from evil.

For the kingdom,
the power and the glory
        are yours,
now and for ever.

Peace be with you.

Our union with God and with one another gives us strength. Alone, our edges would fray and unravel, but together we are sturdy.

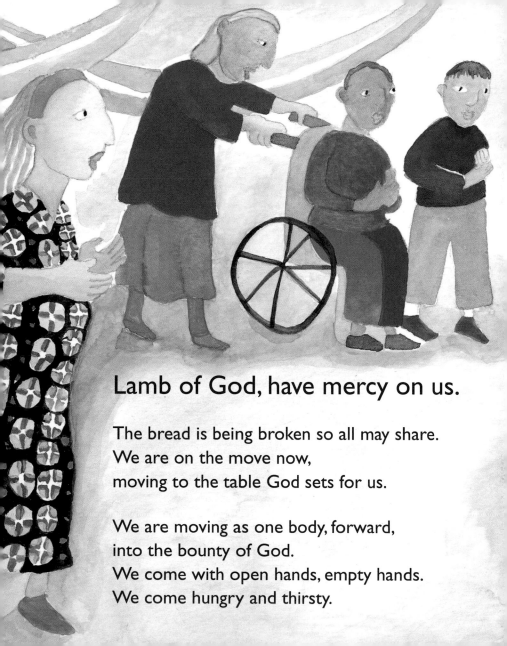

Lamb of God, have mercy on us.

The bread is being broken so all may share.
We are on the move now,
moving to the table God sets for us.

We are moving as one body, forward,
into the bounty of God.
We come with open hands, empty hands.
We come hungry and thirsty.

Lord, I am not worthy
that you should enter
            under my roof,
but only say the word
and my soul shall be healed.

We come to be fed with bread and wine
that have become for us the Body and Blood
of our Lord Jesus Christ.

We come with our hearts open
to receive the Body and Blood of Christ.

We receive the bread and eat it.

We receive the cup in our hands
and drink from it.

The Body of Christ. Amen.
The Blood of Christ. Amen.

We come singing together:

Taste and see,
  taste and see
      the goodness
          of the Lord.

When all have tasted the goodness of the Lord,
then we keep a quiet time.
We think of the wondrous life of God in us,
in this church that has shared the holy banquet.

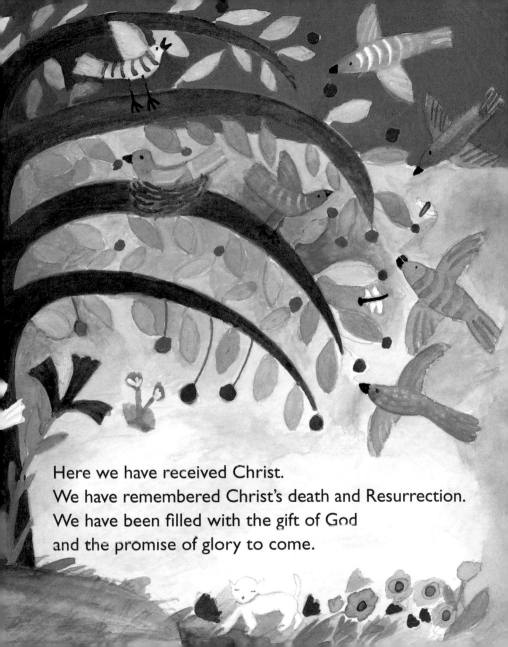

Here we have received Christ.
We have remembered Christ's death and Resurrection.
We have been filled with the gift of God
and the promise of glory to come.

Go and announce the Gospel of the Lord.

We have been blessed. We have been fed.
We are all sung out. We go out.
I will do my work. You will do your work.

We will pray.
We will visit the sick.
We will feed the hungry.

We will clothe the naked.
We will shelter the homeless.
We will teach. We will learn.

We will forgive.
We will ask forgiveness.
We will listen.
We will speak truth.
We will show mercy.
We will do peace.

teach and learn

pray

shelter the homeless

we will go out

visit the sick

clothe the naked

we will do our work

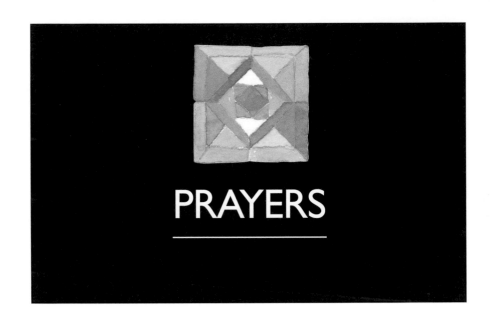

PRAYERS

For Sunday

When you tell about yourself, what do you say?
Do you say, "I am in the second grade at my school"?
Or do you say, "I have a little brother"? Or "I play
the piano"? A creed is a way we tell about ourselves
as the Church. We are the people who hope in God.
This Creed says what we believe about God.

I believe in God,
the Father almighty,
   Creator of heaven and earth.
and in Jesus Christ, his only Son, our Lord,
who was conceived by the Holy Spirit,
born of the Virgin Mary,
suffered under Pontius Pilate,
was crucified, died and was buried;
he descended into hell;
on the third day he rose again from the dead;
he ascended into heaven,
and is seated at the right hand of God
      the Father almighty;
from there he will come to judge the living
      and the dead.

I believe in the Holy Spirit,
the holy catholic Church,
the communion of saints,
the forgiveness of sins,
the resurrection of the body,
and life everlasting. Amen.

We are the people God loves. We are the people God forgives. We call upon God's mercy in this prayer:

I confess to almighty God,
and to you, my brothers and sisters,
that I have greatly sinned,
in my thoughts and in my words,
in what I have done and in what I have failed to do,
[And, striking the breast, say,]
through my fault, through my fault,
through my most grievous fault;
[Then continue with]
therefore I ask blessed Mary ever-Virgin,
all the Angels and Saints,
and you, my brothers and sisters,
to pray for me to the Lord our God.

Before we receive Holy Communion, we can say this prayer:

Soul of Christ, sanctify me.
Body of Christ, heal me.
Blood of Christ, drench me.
Water from the side of Christ, wash me.

This hymn begins with the angels' words at Christ's birth:

Glory to God in the highest,
and on earth peace to people of good will.

We praise you
we bless you,
we adore you,
we glorify you,
we give you thanks for your great glory,
Lord God, heavenly King,
O God, almighty Father.

Lord Jesus Christ, Only Begotten Son,
Lord God, Lamb of God, Son of the Father,
you take away the sins of the world,
    have mercy on us;
you take away the sins of the world,
    receive our prayer;
you are seated at the right hand of the Father,
    have mercy on us.

For you alone are the Holy One,
you alone are the Lord,
you alone are the Most High,
Jesus Christ,
with the Holy Spirit,
in the glory of God the Father.
Amen.

Morning Prayers

We begin each morning tracing the sign of who we are, the sign of the cross. We make the sign: Now down, from head to heart; now across, from shoulder to shoulder.

Once we were baptized in the name of the Father and of the Son and of the Holy Spirit. We remember our baptism every morning when we say:

In the name of the Father, and of the Son, and of the Holy Spirit. Amen.

We thank God for every gift of the new day:

Lord, open my lips, and my mouth will proclaim your praise.

Glory to the Father, and to the Son, and to the Holy Spirit: as it was in the beginning, is now, and will be for ever. Amen.

While we are dressing, we say:

Blessed are you, Lord, God of all creation:
you clothe the naked.

When we are ready to go outside, we say:

Blessed are you, Lord, God of all creation:
you guide my footsteps.

Before we eat breakfast, we make the Sign of the Cross
and we say:

Bless us, O Lord,
and these thy gifts
which we are about to receive
from thy bounty.
Through Christ our Lord.
Amen.

When we have finished, we say:

Blessed be the Lord,
of whose bounty we have received
and by whose goodness we live.

Daytime Prayers

Many times during the day, we pray very short prayers.

Come, Lord Jesus!

Thanks be to God!

May the Lord bless us and keep us.

**Our help is in the name of the Lord,
who made heaven and earth.**

At noon, we ask Mary to pray for us.

**Hail Mary, full of grace,
the Lord is with thee.
Blessed are thou among women,
and blessed is the fruit of thy womb, Jesus.
Holy Mary, Mother of God,
pray for us sinners,
now and at the hour of our death.
Amen.**

Dinner Prayers

We can sing one of these blessings to a familiar tune,
a tune like "Praise God from whom all blessings flow."

Be present at our table, Lord.
Be here and everywhere adored.
Thy creatures bless and grant that we
may feast in Paradise with thee.

We thank thee, Lord, for this our food.
For life and health and every good.
By thine own hand may we be fed:
Give us each day our daily bread.

Or this blessing:

All the world hopes in you, O Lord,
that you will give us food in our hunger.
You open wide your hand
and we are filled with good things.

Evening Prayer

Christians have long sung Mary's song (see Luke, chapter one) as their evening prayer.

My soul proclaims the Lord my God.
My spirit sings God's praise,
Who looks on me, and lifts me up,
That gladness fills my days.

All nations now will share my joy;
For gifts God has outpoured.
This lowly one has been made great.
I magnify the Lord.

For those who fear the Holy One,
God's mercy will not die.
Whose strong right arm puts down the proud,
And lifts the lowly high.

God fills the hungry with good things,
And sends the rich away;
The promise made to Abraham
Is filled to endless day.

Night Prayers

The Bible says God is like a mother bird who
covers her babies with her wings to keep them safe.

We may be afraid in the dark, but we are not alone.
God is with us.

Like a loving mother or a kind father, like a strong
grandparent who comes to care for us when we are ill
in the night, God stays by our side.

We pray for our families and our friends.
We pray for the poor. We pray for the sick.
We name them and ask God to bless each one.
We pray for the dead.

**Eternal rest grant unto them, O Lord,
and let perpetual light shine upon them.
May their souls
and the souls of all the faithful departed,
through the mercy of God, rest in peace.
Amen.**

We ask God's angels to be with us all night and all day.

**Angel sent by God to guide me,
be my light and walk beside me;
be my guardian and protect me;
on the paths of life direct me.**

We end our day as we began our day,
making the sign of the cross.

**Protect us, Lord, as we stay awake;
watch over us as we sleep,
that awake, we may keep watch with Christ,
and asleep, rest in his peace.**

Now it is time to close your eyes. Sometimes your parent
will make the sign of the cross on your forehead and say:

May the Lord bless you and keep you.